Kindle Me a Riddle

ROBERTA KARIM

Kindle Me

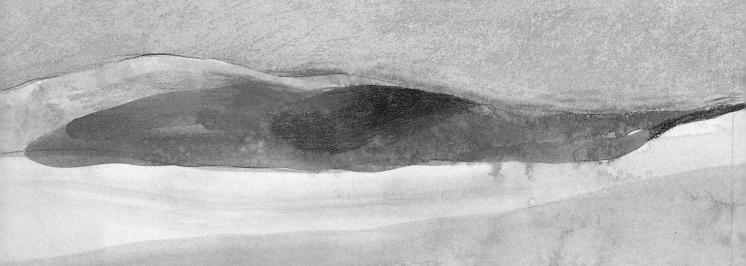

a Riddle

A PIONEER STORY

Pictures by

BETHANNE ANDERSEN

Greenwillow Books • New York

A NOTE FROM THE ARTIST

You can smell hope on a hillside above the Salt Lake Valley in early April, canyon wind from melting snow coming across the budding trees. That is what my great-grandmother sensed each spring after a long winter. That breeze gave five generations of my family a home in the West.

The paintings in this book were inspired by the landscape of eastern Utah, and set in the late 1850s. Special thanks to Assistant Professor Ellen Baker at Columbia University for her careful attention to the text and art, Carma DeJong Anderson, who knows what my ancestors wore, and Cathy Quinton, Curator of Education at This Is the Place Heritage Park in Salt Lake City, who knows how they lived and what was in their homes.

—B. A. A.

Oil paints on a gesso background were used to prepare the full-color art.
The text type is Leawood Medium.

Text copyright © 1999 by Roberta Karim
Illustrations copyright © 1999 by Bethanne Andersen
www.williammorrow.com
Printed in Singapore by Tien Wah Press
First Edition
10 9 8 7 6 5 4 3 2 1   SEP 1 '99

Library of Congress Cataloging-in-Publication Data
Karim, Roberta.
Kindle me a riddle: a pioneer story / by Roberta Karim; pictures by Bethanne Andersen.
p. cm.
Summary: The riddles that a pioneer family share explain the origin of such things in their lives as their log cabin, johnnycakes, the broom, a cloak, candles, and more.
ISBN 0-688-16203-7 (trade).   ISBN 0-688-16204-5 (lib. bdg.)
[1. Frontier and pioneer life—Fiction.   2. Family life—Fiction.   3. Riddles—Fiction]
I. Andersen, Bethanne, (date) ill.   II. Title.
PZ7.K1384Ki   1999   [E]—dc21   98-18955   CIP   AC

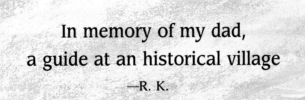

In memory of my dad,
a guide at an historical village
—R. K.

To my father,
for making the Wild West fit into my heart
—B. A. A.

'Papa and I walked down
the wagon road, carrying coals
from Neighbor Drake's fire.
Our cabin was still
a half-mile away.
Our icy cold cabin.
And it was my fault.
A tear skittled down my nose.
"Papa," I whispered, "I'm sorry
I let the fire die."
"Shucks," said Papa,
patting my nose dry.
"Want to hear a riddle?"
"Oh, yes," I said.

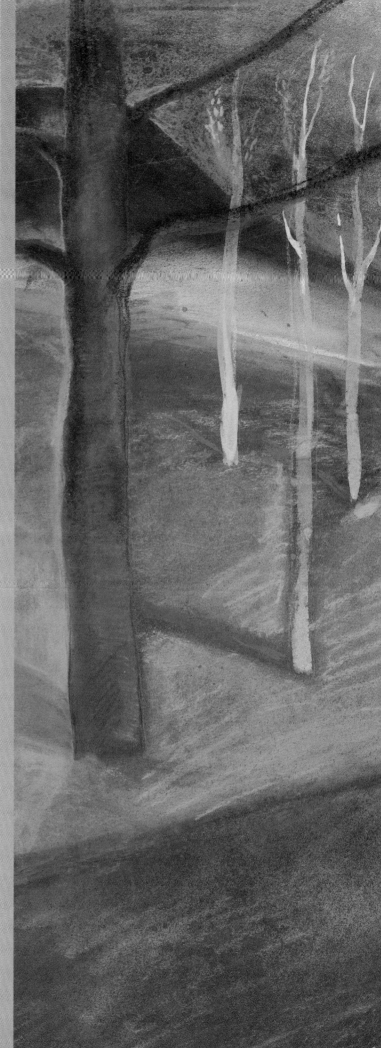

"Oh, dear," said Papa.

"Let me think."

He scratched his beard. "Aha!

What is a wagon road," he asked,

"before it's a wagon road?"

I frowned. "Was it not always

a wagon road?"

"No, daughter Constance.

Give up?"

"Yes."

"It was a buffalo trail,

long and deep!" he said.

I stood still to imagine.

We came near our cabin.
"Papa, I have a riddle for you!
What is a log cabin
before it's a log cabin?"
He set down the kettle
and lifted me high.
"Tall pine trees that sheltered
the forest floor?" he asked.
"Good answer!" I said.

I hopped in the chilly cabin
and twizzled Jack's hair.
"Mama, listen! Papa has a riddle
for you!"
"I do?" asked Papa.
He blew on our neighbor's coals
until they glowed red hot and
caught our kindling on fire.
"Fair enough," he said.
"Trade you a riddle for breakfast?"
Mama gave him a cold johnnycake.
Papa gave her a riddle. "What is
johnnycake before it's johnnycake?"
"Work?" asked Mama.
"No!" I said, twirling my petticoats.
"Ears of corn shucked
at the husking bee frolic!"

Bubbling hot hominy
warmed us through.
Jack raised his mug and asked,
"What is our cider before it's cider?"
Papa tooted on the jug.
I sang along,
"Apples bobbing up and down
out in the orchard."
"Then *bob* to your partner,"
Papa called out.
We linked elbows
and circled like cyclones.
The wooden boards clattered.

Mama said, "We're done now,"
and handed Jack a broom.
"But *I'm* not done," he said,
and grinned. "What is a broom
before it's a broom?"
Papa swept Jack,
and Jack swept the floor.
"Achoo!" I said. "A broom?
A birch branch,
sweeping clouds away."

The dancing flame
warmed Papa's hands.
"A red-hot fire we kindled,
Constance."
"Red-hot riddles, too!" I said.
Papa went out to look for rushes,
then leaned back in to say,
"What is a fireplace
before it's a fireplace?"
Mama smiled. "I remember.
Round shiny stones
in the bubbling stream."

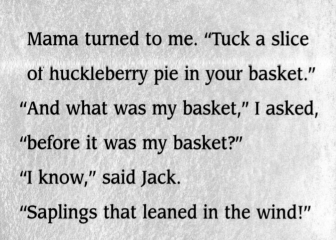

Mama turned to me. "Tuck a slice of huckleberry pie in your basket."
"And what was my basket," I asked, "before it was my basket?"
"I know," said Jack.
"Saplings that leaned in the wind!"

"These riddles light faster
than kindling," said Mama.
"Go now, riddlers.
You'll be late for school."
"But I have the perfect one,"
said Jack.
"Constance, what was your winter
cloak before it was your cloak?"
I laughed, remembering.
"It belonged to another.
'Twas the sheep's winter cloak!"

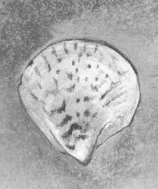

At school we put our toes
on the line and recited our ABC's.
Then we pulled out slates and chalk.
My brother raised his hand.
"What is our chalk
before it's our chalk?"
"Why, Jack," said Miss Larsen,
"what a good question."
I chuckled in my sleeve.
Our teacher answered,
"Chalk comes from seashells
pressed tightly together."

After school we leapfrogged home,
riddles bouncing in our heads.
Time for the evening chores.
"Constance, run to the springhouse
for a crock of butter, please."
Jack tagged along
and hid behind the icehouse.
"What are ice blocks
before they're ice blocks?" he said.
"Don't you know?" I asked.
"Yes," he said. "Pond water
splashing in the sun."
"*You* were the one
who was splashing," I said.

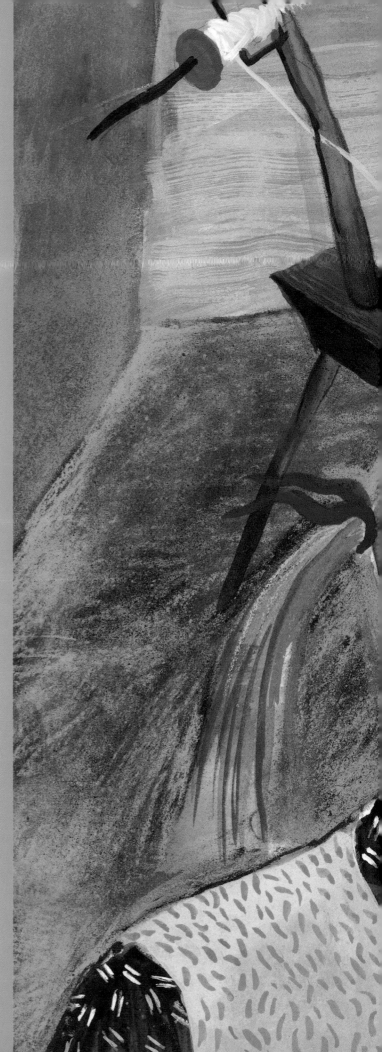

After supper we sat
close to the sizzling fire.
Papa wove rushes
and Mama spun flax.
"What is my sampler
before it's my sampler?" I asked.
Papa raised an eyebrow.
"Still at it, Constance?
You are rightly named!
How many riddles
have you kindled today?"
I laughed. "Maybe one or two . . .
hundred?"
Mama said, "Your sampler?
Flax in the fields,
growing straight and tall,
spun on the spinning wheel,
woven on the loom."

The light flickered low
on my stitches.
Papa put down his rushes
and picked up a book.
We all settled down to listen.
After the story Jack popped up.
"What's an eventide candle
 before it's a candle?"
"Beeswax," I said,
"from the bright honeycomb."

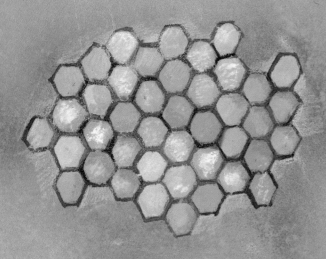

The coals were red hot.

I banked the fire.

"How's this, Papa? No more

icy cold mornings."

Papa gave me a hug.

"Tomorrow we shall kindle

a blazing fire."

"Tonight . . ." I said, "kindle me

a riddle, Papa. Just one more?"

"One more?" he said. "Very well."

"What are your mattress and pillow

before they're your mattress

and pillow?"

"A sweet field of yellow straw,"

said Jack, and yawned.

"Downy feathers from my ducks

and geese," I said, and yawned.

We climbed to the loft.

I peeked over. "One more riddle?"

"One!" growled Papa.

"What is my doll before it's my doll?"

I asked.

Mama whispered, "Corn husks

dancing in the cool moonlight.

Now . . . good-night!"

THE LIFE OF A PIONEER FAMILY

How hard was life for a pioneer family? Imagine yourself at the log cabin. Hours of hard work, sometimes tedious, sometimes backbreaking, go into each drop of morning cider, each drip of eventide candle. But your family has fun, too, with such things as "apple bees," handmade toys, and word games. Would you like to have lived back then? Read on!

FIRE IN THE FIREPLACE

For a pioneer family in a log cabin, the fire in their fireplace was extremely important. It cooked their food, gave them light, and kept them warm. At bedtime the fire had to be banked into a heap of coals, or it would die during the night and the family would wake to an icy cold cabin. *(Page 6)*

THE WAGON ROAD

The first roads were made by animals: wolves, bears, and especially buffalo. Herds of buffalo trampled trails on their way to new pastures. Native Americans followed these trails, hunting the buffalo, which gave them food, clothing, and shelter. Later, pioneers moving westward followed the same trails, but they chopped down trees on either side so their covered wagons could get through. *(Page 8)*

COALS FROM THE NEIGHBOR

There were two ways to re-start the fire. The family could strike flint rock against steel, making a spark. With luck the spark caught a dry leaf on fire. Then small twigs called kindling were added, and bit by bit the fire grew. The second way to re-start the fire? Borrow some red-hot chunks of wood, called coals, from the neighbors' fire—if they didn't live too far away! These coals were carried by kettle back to the hearth, fed with kindling, and soon a fire was blazing. *(Page 6)*

A STONE FIREPLACE

As the family prepared to build their cabin, they also gathered stones from a nearby stream to make a large fireplace. But they did not build a stone chimney. They needed shelter quickly, so they built a temporary stick-and-mud chimney, which sometimes caught on fire. Later they built a beautiful stone chimney. *(Page 18)*

THE LOG CABIN

Before a pioneer family built their log cabin, they lived in their covered wagon. Neighbors came to help with the "house raising." But sometimes there were no neighbors. Then the family worked alone, chopping down tall trees (and often dragging them a long distance), notching logs, and stacking them. Creek mud and bits of wood filled the gaps. Boards from their covered wagon became the roof and door. Windows were first covered with animal skins. Eventually, the family obtained oiled paper or glass. *(Page 10)*

THE NECESSARY BROOM

Whittling one end of a birch branch into strips created the bristle end of a broom. A broom could also be made by tying straw to a stick. Brooms were important to a pioneer household, not only for sweeping the floor but also for sweeping up fireplace ash. Ashes were saved in a big barrel. Hot water poured through the ashes made lye. Then the lye was stirred with animal fat for three to five hours to make the family's soap. *(Page 16)*

THE APPLE ORCHARD

Settlers brought along young fruit trees and planted their own orchards. The land was rich, and the trees grew swiftly. Neighbors came together for an "apple bee" to process the harvest. Apples could be sliced and dried near the fire, cooked into apple butter, or pressed into cider. Families often drank apple, pear, or peach cider with their meals. *(Page 14)*

CHALK AND SLATES

Long ago, sea water and mud pressed tiny seashells on the ocean floor into chalk. Great heat and pressure on fine-grained rock caused slate to be formed. Slate splits easily into thin, smooth sheets. Pioneer students used sheets of slate instead of paper, and chalk instead of pencils. They also wrote on pieces of bark with sticks that had been burned at the sharpened end. *(Page 24)*

CORN AND MORE CORN

Shucking ears of corn alone was boring, so neighbors gathered at harvest time for a "husking bee" frolic. Everyone shucked corn, then ate and danced together. Corn ground into cornmeal was used in many recipes, including corn bread or johnnycake. Cornmeal mush, called hominy, was cooked in a kettle and made a hot, hearty meal. *(Page 12)*

CLOAKS

In the springtime, pioneers fortunate enough to have a sheep or two sheared the sheep's winter wool. The wool was washed, carded back and forth on wire brushes in order to untangle and collect the fibers, spun into yarn on a spinning wheel, then knit or woven into warm garments, such as cloaks. Cloaks were long capes, and were often worn instead of coats. *(Page 22)*

BOOKS

The pioneer mother was her children's first teacher of the "3 R's." Using a stick, she drew the letters and numbers in the fireplace ashes to teach Reading, 'Riting, and 'Rithmetic. If there were any books in the cabin, they were often the family Bible and, from 1836 on, a McGuffey Reader. *(Page 30)*

THE SPRINGHOUSE

Pioneer families needed water for drinking, cooking, and washing. So before they built a cabin, they made sure there was a pond, river, or spring nearby. Settlers liked springs because they could build a little log or stone house over the icy water. This springhouse was used as a kind of refrigerator to keep the milk and butter cool. And ice blocks, cut from a frozen pond, stacked in straw, and stored in an icehouse, kept food cool even into the summer. *(Page 26)*

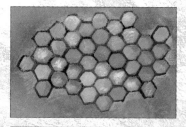

CANDLES

When darkness fell each night, the family could no longer work outside. They ate their supper, then sat down by the fireplace. The light from the fire was sufficient for most activities: spinning, whittling, or weaving chair seats from marsh plants called rushes. But for close work like reading or stitching a sampler, more light was needed, and the family sometimes lit a precious candle. Candles were made by dipping string wicks into beeswax or animal fat over and over again. *(Page 30)*

SAMPLERS

Since everything was hand sewn by women at home, it was important that girls learn to sew well. As a form of training, each young girl carefully stitched the alphabet and numbers onto a linen cloth. This sampler took many, many hours to complete. Often the finished masterpiece was framed and hung on the wall. *(Page 28)*

BASKETS

Baskets were handy for carrying everything from berries to lunches. Baskets began with young trees called saplings. The father cut down a sapling with an ax, then split it along its length into halves, quarters, and finally eighths. With his knife, he sliced the eighths into long strips of wood. These strips were woven together to make baskets. *(Page 20)*

CORN-HUSK DOLLS

Pioneer children had very few toys. They might have played with a wooden slingshot, a ball-and-cup, or a spinning top. Boys knew how to whittle a fish hook. Girls knew how to make dolls from rags with dried apple faces, or from colorfully dyed corn husks. *(Page 34)*

MAKING CLOTH

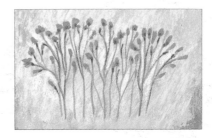

The pioneer family made winter clothes out of wool but summer clothes out of linen. Linen started out as flax, growing in the fields. When the flax plants were cut down, their stems were soaked in water and beaten. As the stems were pulled through the sharp nails of a hackle (a board or comb with metal teeth), many fibers were trapped. These fibers were spun into thread on a spinning wheel, then woven into linen cloth on a loom. *(Page 28)*

A MATTRESS AND A PILLOW

The pioneer's bed was a few hard boards or a wooden frame with ropes. To make the bed more comfortable, straw was stuffed between two pieces of cloth and sewn up as a mattress. Pillows were stuffed with feathers from ducks, chickens, or geese. Children had no bedrooms of their own. Sometimes they slept in trundle beds pulled out at night from under their parents' bed. Sometimes they slept by the fire on mattresses unrolled for the night. And sometimes they climbed the ladder to the loft, curled up between straw mattresses and warm bearskins or other coverings, and fell asleep. *(Page 32)*

W24   A 9/11/00
LC

DISCARD